The Home Party Sales Consultant's BIG Idea Book:

Tons of tips for getting your name out, finding leads, bonus & incentive programs, party themes, game ideas, recruiting suggestions, filing taxes, and more!

SARAH MAKOWSKY

DEDICATION

"If you find a path with no obstacles, it probably doesn't lead to anywhere." ~Frank Clark

I dedicate this book to my wonderful family who has helped me with every obstacle along the way. I am lucky to have each of you in my life.

CONTENTS

1

The Sky is the Limit

You went to a home show not expecting to buy much, but then you fell in love with the products, signed some papers, and WHAM you are now the proud owner of a home business. When you wake up the morning after the party, you may feel like you are waking up with a hangover as you wonder, "what have I done?!?" Especially when you try to muster up the enthusiasm to explain the new business venture that you've signed up for to your not so enthusiastic and downright unimpressed husband.

If your husband's cynicism has you second guessing your decision, rest assured you have made a good choice. You are in the right place at the right time. With the fast paced stressful lifestyles of today, many people turn to the internet for after hours shopping from home. Another side effect of today's hectic lifestyle is that it leaves women disconnected and longing for girlfriend time. So a home party show fills two modern needs: shopping and girlfriend time. It is a concept that was destined to succeed. Maybe that is why the direct party home sales industry is growing so rapidly. According to the IRS tax records from 2005, an estimated 13.3 million people nationwide and over 47.3 million people worldwide that have decided to enter the home party direct sales industry.

It seems like a new direct sale business opens every day. It used to be that Tupperware was in a league of its own and the Tupperware parties were pretty much the only home party company on the scene. But those days of dominance are gone. Tupperware began breaking off into many different subsidiaries set up to target diverse markets. Other companies ran to get in the game. Now there are companies that specialize in everything from spa, make-up, home specialty products, children's books, scrapbooking, stamping and so much more. If you can dream it, there is probably already a direct sale company that already sells it.

All of this makes it easier than ever to find a company (or several companies) that sell products you love. Becoming a consultant for the company gives you a great opportunity to get the products at great discounts.

Plus when your friends and family love it too, you have a great opportunity for part-time income.

So even if the fast talking home party consultant that signed you up started to make you feel like a used car buyer with her smooth talking well rehearsed speech about how rosy things will be for you and how much money you will make with her company, don't feel like you were duped. The truth is, if you are careful and do your research so you can avoid falling into common pitfalls, you can get a lot for a very low cash investment. This book will give you all kinds of tips and suggestions for managing your time wisely and making the most of your business in a short time. Most important, it will give you the tools you need to advertise yourself and your business with enthusiasm.

You were smart to enter this booming market. Sales are setting new records every year. New people are constantly signing up. There are so many opportunities for you if you know how to take advantage of them. So where do you begin? The first place to start is with your own mind, because positive thinking is a powerful thing.

This is a business where the sky is the limit. It's all about your attitude and outlook on life. You know that old saying: "Smile and the world smiles with you." There is a reason that saying has been around a long time--- there is a lot of truth behind it! Your attitude really does shape the way your life goes. When you start the day angry and upset and sure that things will be bad all day, you pass that bad vibe on to your husband and children. Now they will immediately start acting the same way. Your prediction comes true: things WILL be bad all day!

I learned this important life lesson in my first job after graduating college. I worked as a loan officer. Being a young twenty-year-old graduate fresh out of college, I was anxious to take on the world and make everyone happy. A people pleaser at heart, I was overly optimistic that I could make everything better. My favorite aspect of my job was helping people who were in over their heads find a practical solution that would help get them back on their feet. I loved to listen to their situation, look at their debts, and find a way to consolidate, stop this pattern, and get things on track.

I quickly learned that nobody wanted to take the time to listen to my advice or suggestions. They wanted money and they wanted it YESTERDAY! This brings me to the hardest part of my job-- dealing with irate clients who were desperate for a loan. They had worked themselves into a jam and wanted nothing but to immediately walk out of my office with a check in their hands for yet another unsecured loan they would never be able to pay. When I told them that there was no way we could offer them another unsecured loan with the amount of debts they already had but that I would love to help them look for another solution that would fit their needs-- perhaps a home equity loan to consolidate their debts--- they would typically fly into a rage.

They would do one of two things: either they would start to cry and tell me how now they would have their home, car, and children taken from them and their life was over; or they would start yelling at me about how stupid I was and demand to speak to a manager.

As you can imagine, neither of these approaches was very helpful and certainly didn't get them out of their current situation. The minute they began attacking me, my desire to help them was over. And the criers, who told me how horrible things were and that there was no way out of the disaster, were too caught up in their pity party to stop using emotion and start using reason to get out of the situation. The few people who came to me saying, "I'm in a jam and need you to help me figure a way out" were the clients that made the job worthwhile. They were thinking positive: there is a way out and I just need to find it.

I am not alone in my desire to help people out. The desire to be needed and helpful is one of the most basic human needs. Always expect the best of everyone and assume they want to help you---not that they are out to get you. Most people do not get pleasure out of trying to mess up your life, so try to start going into new situations with a happy and confident outlook. It will make all the difference in the world.

The next time you are on the phone trying to resolve an issue and feel yourself starting to get frustrated and angry, just try smiling! You're just on the phone and nobody can see you anyways, so try planting a big smile on your face! I bet you'll feel calmer right away. Assume that the person on the other end is willing to listen and help you. And just as important, be willing to listen to them and their suggestions. Chances are they will try to help you, and without a doubt you will be much more successful using this approach than the negative one.

You may be asking how all this relates to your direct sale business. Believe me, it does! Negative thinking spoils every opportunity in your life and destines you for failure. If you think you are not good enough or smart enough to sell the products, you won't be. If you think you are bad at sales, you will be. If you think you are wasting your time and money, you are.

So instead dream and imagine the possibilities, then make those dreams a reality. Set goals and post them where you can see them so you can review them constantly. All you need is desire, self motivation and (perhaps most important) a good attitude. So set your sights on the stars!

I was at training seminar and one of the leaders, who has made a fortune in the direct sales business, really drove home this point with the following visualization. She asked for a volunteer to stand up for a demonstration. The volunteer was asked to close her eyes and raise both arms out to each side like airplane wings. With her arms still outstretched, she was told to think of the most awful and negative world where nothing went her way. As the speaker continued telling the volunteer how horrible things were going for her, she put her hands on each of the volunteer's arms and gave them a slight push. Her arms quickly fell to her side.

"Now, said the speaker, think of a perfect spot where everyone is on your side, everything goes your way and you are just having an unbelievably perfect day." As she relayed the tale of how wonderful life was going for the now lucky volunteer, she again pushed her arms to make them fall. But this time they didn't budge. They stayed out straight, strong, and firm. It was a powerful image of the power of positive thinking. The speaker finished by saying that it works every single time. I went home and tried it on my husband. She's right… it works every time

2

Sparking Interest:
Enthusiasm Is Contagious

You have something that you love and can't wait to show to the world. The best thing to do in the beginning when you are excited about the company, the product, and your new opportunity, is to get out there and tell everyone you can about it. Call your friends and family first to share your excitement. "You are not going to believe the wonderful products I saw demonstrated last night. They are going to make such a difference in my life. I couldn't wait to get them home to try them out. In fact I loved them so much I've decided to become a distributor." Your enthusiasm will be contagious and your friends will be interested and will probably love to help you get started and see you reach your goals. So start getting small groups together for demonstrations. This is a great time to do one-on-one personal "shows" for friends and family that will lead to future shows.

Don't be shy talking about your products or business! If you genuinely love your products, others will be interested too so don't be afraid to **ASK, ASK, ASK!!!** The worst someone can say is "no thanks!" But you'll be amazed at the number of people who will say "yes" when you are friendly, excited and enthusiastic. You are in control of the way people react to you. When you are confident and obviously excited and interested in what you have to show, potential clients will also be interested!

When you are doing these initial personal shows and trying to create interest remember that you have to give a lot to get a lot. In the beginning, you may have to put a lot of energy into getting your name out and you may need to spend a bit on free samples to get people hooked. Just remember that it will work! Don't start by asking for everything, start by giving a lot! For example you may start with a baby step like getting them to try a new lipstick sample and develop a relationship from there. The most important thing in sales is to be responsive and understanding of your client's needs and put those first. Obviously, not everyone wants or needs what you provide and you want to be sure to stop short of becoming an annoyance. The other thing is that people can spot a fake right away and start to feel like you are just looking for your next sale. You have to genuinely like your products and be interested in helping others learn about what you sell to succeed.

I've had people approach me and once they find out my name, use it 30 times in the conversation. Obviously they've heard that people like to be remembered and like to be addressed by their name. But this overkill gives the opposite impression. I've also had people so concerned with their rehearsed speech that they are unresponsive to my concerns. Once a lady was talking and talking about her products. When I finally got a chance to speak to tell her that I'm allergic to the product, she didn't even acknowledge or seem to care about my concerns. She went right on with her sales pitch. This indifference to me made me completely indifferent to her and her products. So you have to strike the right balance to come off as you intend. If this doesn't come naturally to you, enlist friends to help you practice and tell them not to be easy on you! Once you're confident and ready to introduce people to your products, start brainstorming on every avenue where you can advertise and promote yourself. Do everything you can to get your name out there!

Advertising can make or break your business, so find ways to get your name out everywhere you go! There are a lot of low budget ways you can advertise your business. Start with yourself; you are your own best promotion. Your enthusiasm and love of your products will rub off on everyone, so try to find ways to work your new business into conversations with everyone you meet. Use the products yourself at home, and let people see you using them at the office and while you are out running errands. This is always the best form of advertising anyways! Think about it—are people more likely to buy something because the owner of the company puts out a commercial that says it is great or because their friend uses it and raves about it? The friends review, of course! So use your products every chance you get.

If you sell make-up, you can casually plant a seed in co-workers head in the break room before you go back to work. As you are talking and getting ready to go back to work, pull out your company's lipstick and compact to refresh your make-up. If you sell kitchen products and happen to be going to a potluck dinner, bring a recipe that uses one of your company's tools or is presented on one of your company's nice serving trays. While you are out running errands, wear a shirt or sweatshirt promoting your product or you can put an "ASK ME" button on our purse or coat. These are great conversation pieces that will get the ball rolling. You will be surprised the interest you can generate.

Although you do not want to lose focus of your most important goal-- sparking interest and following leads-- you will need a few business supplies to help get your name out in the community. Don't spend time re-inventing the wheel and creating new marketing tools, mailers, invitations & promotions. www.homebusinessmakeover.com has a huge assortment of tools designed specifically for home party consultants that does all this for you giving you time to spend where it is most important—getting & following leads! So download those templates and then head to the office supply store for business cards and sticky sided label paper (like the kind used to print stickers). Also pick up magnet paper (found in the section with photo paper and photo printing supplies) Print catchy customized business cards to leave everywhere you go. Your name will always be at the tip of their finger. Print contact information labels with the label sheets. These can be stuck to everything from backs of product guides to backs of products samples.

Then the only way to find new customers is to LOOK, so start looking for leads everywhere you go. Never leave home without business cards and never leave a place or area without leaving at least 5 behind. Hand them out personally, or place them in the bathroom, in empty shopping carts at the grocery store, on car windshields. Post business cards or brochures on bulletin boards at stores. Ask to place them at coffee shops, children's resale shops, laundry mats, dry cleaners, and all the places where your children take dance, swim, or gymnastics lessons. Include them in your bills each month. Drop your business card in give away boxes. You never know who is going to look at them and need or want what you have to offer.

You can add a personal touch by wrapping a small sample in tulle and attaching a business card with ribbon. Give one to your banker when you go to the teller, the receptionist at your doctor's or dentist's office, your checker at the grocery store, leave them with a tip for your waitress. Many churches and cities have women's groups that pass out welcome bags to new members, so offer to place your samples and brochures in their care packets. Also ask them about getting a list of new people to move in to the city. They may be looking for a new consultant or new job in your area. You may also check into setting up a display at craft fairs or mall events. Advertise in your church bulletin, your alumni newsletter, and the local newspaper.

Mail out samples, catalogs, and a wish list to everyone you can think of who may be interested. Send a catalog to a co-worker that has moved, and friends of yours who have their own home businesses with an offer to hold joint shows or fairs. Post a catalog in the teacher's lounge at your child's school. When you send in teacher gifts, make them from your company!! Post a catalog in the employee lunch room. Give a catalog to the receptionist at your doctor's or dentist's office. Put your current catalog in your neighbor's door along with a 10% off coupon. Leads are everywhere-- you just have to be creative and find them!

Another effective way to help spark interest in the community is through form letters sent to organizations to generate interest. Try to find clubs and groups where you can give your presentation. For example, you may volunteer to be a speaker at the monthly meeting for a local women's group. Think of as many groups as you can (local mom's group, bunco group, co-workers, church bible study group.) Then think of how your services can be of use to them and draft a letter asking to speak at their next meeting. Always consider the audience you are addressing when writing to spark interest in your services. Suppose you sell bath & body products. Here are two examples of how you may change the approach to fit the needs and interest of the group you are addressing. To address a bunco group of woman you may send something like this:

Looking for a fun idea for a Mom's Night Out for your group?
Introducing.... **MARGARITA MANIA!!!**
As hostess you provide the margaritas, guests can bring their favorite appetizer to share. I'll bring the rest for a night of pampering and fun with the girls! We'll start with manicures and pedicures. We will also perform 5 minute makeovers, play a fun lipstick personality game, and experience all kinds of great smelling, stress relieving bath & body products.

Due to the huge popularity of this party, dates are filling fast to contact me today!
To schedule a Mom's Night out for your group call or e-mail.
You can also visit my web page for more info and to schedule your party online!

SPECIAL LIMITED TIME OFFER: When you schedule your girl's night for June or July, EVERY guest gets a FREE 4-IN-1 PEDICURE BRUSH!!

This letter addresses the group in several ways: they are left wanting to know more so they will log on to your web page for more details. It also makes your services seem in demand, and offers a special offer and women love good deals, incentives & special offers. When they e-mail (or mail) you back to say it sounds great...what's the catch? You tell them you are just trying to get your name out in the community and hopefully this will lead to future bookings.

You would take a much different approach to a business. Here is how you may word a request to a health club or business organization:

INTRODUCING <COMPANY NAME>
AND THE TOTAL RENEWAL:

These days everyone is overscheduled, always running and STRESSED! Stress has become a national epidemic with huge consequences to our society. It is so important to remember to make room in our busy schedules every day to nurture our spiritual lives. I specialize in stress management and will provide your group with a Total Renewal that introduces simple stress relief measures they can use every day.

My presentation introduces several products and techniques that are designed to calm, soothe and relax. I have done this presentation for several different groups including: MOMS Club business meetings, MOPS groups, teacher appreciation escapes, BUNCO groups, tennis teams, ladies night out, and church groups. It can be customized to your individual groups needs, but usually is approximately 30 minutes and would include several fun spa quality treatments and a relaxation exercise-- a sample of some stress relief treatments is enclosed.
Best of all, there is no cost or obligation to you--- I am just trying to get our company's name out in the community. There will not be any pressure on anyone to purchase our products. It is a relaxing and fun time. Everyone enjoys them and I usually have several people decide to host their own in home spa renewal.

To schedule a **TOTAL RENEWAL** presentation for your group or to find out more info, please call or e-mail me…. You can also visit my webpage for more info and to schedule your **RENEWAL** online!

Notice the different voice depending on the audience. This letter is very effective because it addresses the organization's concerns. You are giving their clients a free service. It is fun. It is quick. You will not be in the way and pressuring their clients to buy your products.

There are a number of different group parties you can "host" yourself to help you get those first bookings on the calendar. From these you will find your next host, loyal client, and future consultants. So here are several parties that will help you get bookings on your calendar:

One-On-One Themes

Sneak Preview: If someone is interested in finding out more about your products, invite them over for a one-on-one preview of your products. After you've shown her all your products, offer a package deal that is too good to pass up! For instance you may put together a group of 10 bestsellers and offer it at a discount. This is not as much as your new consultant bundle that she would get if she becomes a consultant. You do not want her to feel like all you are interested in doing here is sign her up! You really want to generate interest in your products, so just put together a few things that may add up to about $60 or $70 to thank her and get her hooked on your favorite products.

Individual Image Profile: We'll begin with color analysis to determine your best colors for clothes & make-up. Then we'll determine your customized skin care regimen based on your individual skin care concerns. You'll get great customized advice. **Great for brides to be!**

Charity Themes

Party for a Cause: A set amount of your sales will be donated to the charitable organization near and dear to the heart of your hostesses. The hostess may also choose to have you donate monetary value of the rewards you would have given her as a hostess or may want to donate the actual items (i.e. beauty products to a homeless women's shelter.) Remember you have a bonus for your charitable acts: it's all a tax write off so keep records!

Adopt a Neighbor Find a local needy family (churches are great sources for this) and donate all of the freebie & 1/2 prices items that are earned during this party to the needy family! (A great party especially if a family in your neighborhood has lost their home to fire or some other type of disaster!)

Sponsor a Contest: Organizations are often looking for donations for door prizes for their events. Make up a gift basket of your products that also include a catalog, order sheet, hostess rewards sheet, and sponsoring information. Even if the person who actually receives the basket never contacts you, you were still able to get your name out to many more people for minimal cost. And the others that may have seen your basket may contact you about purchasing one of their own, so be sure to have several business cards lying next to your basket if it will be displayed.

Organization Fundraiser: Organizations are always looking for creative ways to raise money, so choose an organization that you are affiliated with and offer a percentage of the profits go to them. For instance: a book fair for your child's school, or a spa day with a percentage of profits going to your local mothers and tots group.

I Have the Solution Express Themes

Remember that the most successful sellers are experts at listening to and working around their clients problems. So if a potential host seems interested but has reservations, find a solution for her. Don't have time, space, or friends nearby? Here are some solutions:

Nights Too Busy to Party: Do a quick get-together over brunch! Bagels, donuts, a fresh pot of coffee and me! Perfect for a Saturday or Sunday morning. In an hour or two your party will be complete and the rest of the day is yours! Each guest who brings a goodie to share will receive a free gift.

Spa Works: An express escape for groups. This is usually done with 2-4 consultants depending on group size. **Great for church groups, ladies groups, employee lunch breaks, and member appreciation events.** We've done this at health clubs, schools for teacher appreciation events, and for mom's groups. This can be catered to your groups' needs & time constraints but usually includes neck wrap, instant manicure, and mini massages as we take you through a relaxation & visualization experience.

Sitter Party: This is a great party to have, especially if your guest will have small children. Having a sitter present allows mom and dad to shop undisturbed!

Ten to Midnight Party: Do an outdoor party late at night for the guests that cannot make it early in the day.

Moms on the go GYM Party: Contact your LOCAL Fitness Gyms and see if you can come & do a party there for busy moms!

Work Place LUNCH Office Parties: (can also hold them at the workplace after work too!)

Pass the Catalog Party: Many direct sales consultants are reluctant to do a catalog party. Catalog parties are sometimes more convenient to your hostess, therefore you should never discourage a catalog party! Often hostesses will totally just cancel all together if she feels she is being pressured into doing something she does not want to do. If a hostess wants to try a catalog party, allow her to try! If the party turns out successful, she is more likely to agree to a home show in the future

Video Book Order Party: do a demo party & have someone take a Video of it! This is great for NON LOCAL Catalog Parties. It is pretty easy to do this and make a short video that can even be sent as an e-mail.

Online Chat Room Party

Be Your Own Hostess: Can't find a host? Who needs one when you can be your own!

Mystery Hostess Open House Party: Why wait for a hostess? Have an open house at your home and invite all those people who were interested in hosting but didn't have the space, didn't know anyone to invite etc. One lucky person's name will be drawn and they will be the "hostess" and gets all the free hostess rewards for the party!!

Hold an Open House

Have a booth at a school fair

Host an office party or brunch

Host an office lunch at your husband's work

Host a show before or during a PTA meeting

Get a booth at local craft shows & festivals: Use this more for recruiting but also accept orders from those who come just to buy from you! Part of growing your business is getting your business out in front of your community

Hostess Appreciation Tea: When new products come out, get your former hostesses together for a tea/brunch. They have shown interest in the past!

Offer to hold a class for your local grocery store, bank etc.

3

Hostess Coaching Helpers

Now that you've set up the ground work, you'll probably have leads pouring in. The new trick is to keep them interested in the show. If you haven't been doing this long, let me warn you now: you will have a lot of people book shows and cancel or back out (usually at the last minute.) I've heard consultants say that they are afraid to answer the phone the day of their show for fear it is the hostess canceling. Then if the show does hold, they dread hearing the phone ring while they are setting up for fear it is the guests calling to cancel. This happens. And when it does you have to roll with it, but you can take steps to ensure that it happens a lot less frequently.

First, you have to start thinking positive (remember about how you have to "smile and the world will smile with you") When you think everything is going to go wrong, guess what? IT WILL! So assume that everything will go great. You have to keep excited and enthusiastic to keep your hostess & guests excited.

The best way to keep someone excited and interested is to get her to commit to a time not too far in advance and keep reminding her of all her rewards and incentives for hosting. She is your partner and your successful show is a success to her. Many companies offer the hostess a percentage of the sales in the form of products.

Consider offering a bonus gift that she gets to take home when she books a show. This will help keep her committed to holding the show. If you have an item you want to get people hooked on and coming back for (for instance skin care line for spa companies) offer it at your cost to anyone who hosts a show. It is a win-win situation because she will want to host to get the offer, will commit to actually holding the show because she will feel indebted to you since she has already gotten an incentive, and best of all hopefully while she starts using the product she will fall in love with your great products and will come back to re-order again and again.

Now be sure to follow-up and keep in touch and begin building a relationship with your future hostess. Help her find guests and answer both her questions and the guests. You don't want to become a nuisance, but following up and getting guests excited about the show is so important to the success of the show. Plus talking to your hostess and getting to know her helps establish a loyal relationship which helps cut down on cancellations.

It is a good idea to be organized and adopt a regular routine with everyone that books a show. This keeps you from becoming confused over what you've offered to each hostess. Here is a sample procedure to follow up after the hostess has booked:

1. Right away, send a hostess reward sheet (examples are shown in the following section) along with a thank you note thanking the hostess for the party/show/class with the following reminder--Date and Time, and then this note: "I look forward to being your consultant and your partner to help you obtain all the free items you want! I work strictly by appointment and will be there on _____so if for any reason you are unable to hold your appointment please notify me 48 hours in advance so we can reschedule your appointment and I can place another hostess in you slot that may be waiting for an opening. I really appreciate your hosting the _____ (show, class, etc) and look forward to working with you. I know it will be a great success. I will call you in a couple of days to see how many guests will be attending your _____." (The hostess reward sheet that you include should include hostess coaching tips so no need to go further in the card.)

2. Call in a couple of days and check to see how many guests are coming. Get their phone numbers or e-mails so you can contact them and get them interested in the show yourself. See the dish towel game on page 31 for a great excuse for her to call all of her guests!!!

3. About 2 days before the party, call her again to see if she needs help with anything or has any questions. Also check about set up and to see how many outside orders she may have.....(the main reason you are doing this is to make sure she doesn't end up canceling...she's more likely to hold to the show when she knows you are serious, knows you won't reschedule her show, and knows you've called her guests already.)

Once you have a few shows on your calendar, and it's time for your first shows you can switch for a while from looking for leads and focus on making your home parties FUN so that everyone has a good time and will want to book their own shows! Your best tool for recruiting future shows is from your current hostess. Her enthusiasm and excitement (or lack of!!) will wear off on her family and friends. Get to the home show early to set up and offer your hostess YET ANOTHER incentive on top of all the others she is already getting. This one will enlist her to help you with booking future shows.

Tell her that she knows her family and friends better then you do, and ask her to find out who, out of her friends and family, would want to have a show.....
    for the 1st Booking she will receive.... $10 in Free Merchandise
    for the 2nd Booking she will receive.... $25 in Free Merchandise
    for the 3rd Booking she will receive.... $50 in Free Merchandise!

You can also offer that she can be the 3rd Booking when she schedules another show for a few months from now. So if she is able to find all the booking she could be starting her show with $50 in free products on top of all the other gifts she gets for hosting!

At the End of the Show when you are offering your hostess rewards, tell them to talk to the hostess about how rewarding and simple hosting is. "If you are considering booking your own show see our hostess __Name____ she has all the Hostess Packets and can tell you how easy and rewarding hosting really is!"

For this incentive, the hostess will not get the free merchandise until after all the home shows are actually held. The hostess will actually be helping you make sure the shows hold since she wants her cash bonus. Her friends will have to answer to her if they end up not following through on their home show commitment.

When guests see how much the hostess is getting, they want in to! So remember to spoil your hosts (and make sure everyone takes notice!) Highlight your hostess rewards plan at least three times per show. At the beginning of the show ask the hostess to tell why she decided to have a show (if she doesn't already do it for you--mention the hostess goal!) Ask past hostesses at shows to talk about their free products.

Towards the end of the presentation hold up product packages and offer them at huge discounts when guests book a future show. Share upcoming specials, next month's promotions and hostess rewards. Make sure at the end of the show you mention how much the hostess saved by having a show. Even if guests weren't interested in booking a show, make sure all guests leave with a catalog or brochure that includes hostess rewards with your contact information on it. They may just want to think about it and not be pressured right now. Remember to follow up!

Here are 2 more fun sample hostess helpers that help get the hostess motivated right after she books. You may also want to offer the following challenges to your hostess:

Hostess Scavenger Hunt

Here is a list of 21 different kinds of people. If you get ten of them to your party on _____, (day) ___/___/___. I will have a special gift for you. Happy Hunting!!

A red headed lady

A waitress

A neighbor

Someone with all sons

A mother of a baby under 1 year old

A bowler

A lady on a diet

An in-law

A teacher or Sunday School teacher

Someone with no children

A stay-at-home mom

A Pregnant Lady

A Church Friend

A grandmother

Someone with all daughters

Someone who orders $50 or more

A person who decorates cakes

A lady with size 9 shoes

A former neighbor

A club member

Someone who will book a party

Party Hostess
Tic Tac Toe to success!

I rely on word of mouth and referrals to help spread my business, so I believe in spoiling you as a hostess. By the time her show is over, the hostess generally walks away with a total of $185 in gifts and discounts. To thank you for scheduling with me you receive your first gift valued at $25. Check out my hostess rewards so you can plan on getting the most free stuff! Mark off each box as you complete the task. Each tic tac toe you get earns you another prize!

Hostess: _____ Show Date: _____ Time: _____

Have at least 6 people at your party	Your party sales total $250 or more	Book one party BEFORE your own
Complete the hostess information sheet and return within 10 days of your show	Hold your show on originally scheduled date	Ask me about the opportunity to start your own business
Send invitations to at least 20 people	Personally call each guest two days before the show to remind them and get them excited!	Collect $75 in orders BEFORE your show (try those who can't come!)

HOSTING IS AS EASY AS 1-2-3!

1. Give me the name and addresses of your friends, neighbors, co-workers, and relatives that you wish to invite.
2. On the day of your show, keep it simple: Just something to drink and a little chocolate. Extra candles make it extra special.
3. Have fun, relax and earn rewards by playing the tic tac toe to success! **Fill the board and you can also get your customized skin care line for only $35 in addition to your prizes!**

4

Recruiting: Be Willing To
Share The Opportunity

Recruiting is the name of the game for most home business structures. Virtually all of the big name home party sale businesses are multilevel marketing (MLM) companies. In this business structure, consultants are encouraged to recruit other distributors or sales representatives and receive a commission or bonus on the sales made by their underlying consultants. This recruitment of down liners is essential to increase a sales representative's sales force and thus generate a greater number of sales. In addition, many companies allow greater rewards and discounts based on the number of down liners a consultant has.

The best place to recruit is at your shows. Your order of priorities at your home shows should be: **1**. Recruit new consultants **2**.Find new Hostesses **3**.Settle for Sales. Sales are great, but recruiting is what keeps your business going.

At the start of the show, ask each person to introduce themselves, say how they know the hostess, and also think of what they would do with an extra $500 a month. This gives you lots of helpful information to explain how your company can help them meet their dreams. Remember their answers at the end of the show when they are closing the show and have a chance to talk to them one on one about how you can meet their needs. Also be on the lookout for people in situations that would benefit from the home sales opportunity so that you can point out specifics of how your company will help them. Look and see if you notice.......

Party guests who give the most input about your product.
The guest with the largest order.
Guests who ask lots of questions.
People who bring extra guests to a show.

People who nod their head when you give your recruit talk.
Anyone who stares at you during the presentation.
The guest who picks up a product and demonstrates it.
The guest who lingers after the presentation.
People who are not working now but would like to find something to occupy their time.
People who need extra money.
People who are bored in their careers.
Someone who is temporarily out of work (male or female).
Part time worker.
Mothers with small children.
Women whose children have grown.
The person who is naturally attracted to you as a person.
Anyone who needs money or is dissatisfied with their job.
The person who is looking to buy a car or any type of luxury.
People who want promotions at their job.
The person who is kid crazy and needs a night cut.
The person who is 40, middle class, and bored

Make mental notes of these people and when you are closing orders at the end of the show, ask them if they've ever thought of doing what you do. Tell her you are looking for people to join your team and you think she'd be a natural.

Of course, the best way to recruit is to have people see how much fun you are having! Who wouldn't want to join you in the fun?

5

Party Themes

Everyone wants to have fun! When your parties seem fun and in demand, you'll have people lining up to book their own fun party for their friends. No matter how great your hostess rewards are, they alone aren't going to get bookings. Incentives are more the icing on the cake, because nobody is going to bring her friends to a dull sales pitch! They want to have a fun girls night with their friends where everyone laughs and enjoys themselves. When the party incorporates more fun and time for guests to chat and enjoy themselves without feeling pressured to buy, the bookings will be pouring in.

Here are some great party themes & ideas galore to help you get lots of bookings on the calendar!!! While some party themes may be specific to a particular product line or business, most of the suggestions listed can be customized to many different organizations. The possibilities are endless, have fun with this list and let it be a springing board for many more ideas!

Mom's Night Out Themes

Great for Bunco groups, Moms of kids in weekly playgroups, Stay-at-home moms etc.

Spa Escape: Relax and be pampered with a sampling of our best selling bath & body, skin care & make-up products. Spa treatments including neck wrap to relieve muscle tension, back & head massage, instant manicure, foot wrap, and a relaxation & visualization experience.

Margarita Mania: A fun night out with the girls! As hostess you provide the margaritas and I'll bring the fun! We'll experience the all our great spa products, do pedicures, manicures & 5 minute makeovers & a play a fun lipstick personality game.

Extreme Makeover: Advanced skin care and image consultation for up to 4 friends. Everyone leaves with a fresh face and new look. You'll be treated to a facial with our daily skin care products then finish with a makeover.

Naughty Night Gown Contest: Each guest brings their favorite night gown in a paper bag; and tries to match the nightie to the guest.

Girls Night In! Party in your PJS Slumber Party! (no men allowed!)- guests wear robes and slippers and come ready to get ready for bed. Go through skin care product line and let each guest do the complete night time routine.

Romantic Outing Picnic Basket Party: Invite all the girls to the party and learn how to prepare a romantic basket to take their lover on a Picnic!

Best Friends Evening Out: (works best with bath & body products or candle types of parties, or skincare & cosmetics type of parties!)

Quick & Easy Meals Taste Great Party: cook a meal using your products. Works great for neighbors on a week night. Have a babysitter available for during the preparation then when the meal is ready everyone comes to join and eat!

Cooking for a Crowd Party: Just before the holidays find some unique holiday recipes that showcase your products! Have a show (complete with samples) showing everyone how to cook for their holiday crowd (using your products of course!) Consultants for home décor companies can easily be adapted to a decorate your house for the holidays, or decorate for company theme.

Party for Crafters who want to get organized

The Busy Mom Slow Cooker Party: Using a Crock Pot for Meals is becoming Popular again for Moms who lead busy lives! Take advantage of that!

Must Have Gadgets Party: fill in the blank depending on your company... must have spa products, holiday products, kitchen products, scrapbooking products...

Pantry & Kitchen Cabinet Make-Over Party: Or craft room makeover party, jewelry box makeover party, memory album makeover party, bookshelf makeover party....

Movie & a Meal Party

Scrapbookers Storage & Organization Party: great for any company with organization products—Tupperware, creative memories, pampered chef….

Rainy Day Fun Kids Craft Party: (great for those in scrapbooking, paper crafts, felt crafts types of parties) Moms are always looking for things to keep kids busy on snow & rainy days! Invite a playgroup over for some fun ideas! You may charge a small fee to cover craft expenses.

Make Great Treats & Sweets for Bake Sales Party: Busy Moms are always looking for a way to make great treats for all those bake sales! You demo some recipes, kitchen gadgets, ways to transport those treats to the bake sale etc! Works really well with parents of elementary school aged children! You can contact the schools PTA and see if they would be interested in having you come to the school and doing this with the moms after one of their PTA meetings!

Moms on a Budget party: During this type of theme party you ONLY demo items that are $20 or less!

NEW MOMS Time Out Party: Invite all the NEW Mothers to attend your party! New moms need a break so giving them a few hours without the kids is something they look forward to!

Dieting Buddies Party: They say that losing weight is more successful if you have a dieting buddy! So if you sell gourmet foods, natural & healthy supplements, vitamins, or exercise equipment you can start a dieting buddies program that incorporates this type of party into it!

Bring On The Men Party Themes
Some fun ways to include the men in your shows!

MEN ONLY Summer BBQ & Grilling Outdoor Party: Invite the men for an afternoon of football, pizza, soda (or beer) and Your Product. Set up a display and let them shop for Christmas presents during halftime, tell them that when they place a $25 (or whatever) order, you'll wrap the gift for them.

Couples Party: This is a great kind of show to do if you sell adult products. Not only do women enjoy shopping for these kinds of things, men also do.

Couples massage party: Great to demonstrate bath & body products. They demonstrate the products on each other. For a party game, print a reflexology chart off the internet and give to each guest or tell them about the different pressure points. Great audience to introduce your men product lines!

Lovers & Couples Cooking Party focusing on Sweet Desserts

MEN Only Cooking Party!

Learn to make Sweet Treats for your Mate

Sports Themed Tailgating Party Super Bowl BASH party

Wine Tasting Party:(make sure you check with your company first to make sure its okay to have alcoholic beverages at your party.) While Guests are "wine tasting" you can do a party for Tupperware, pampered chef, home décor company etc.

Taste of <Company Name> Cooking Party for Couples

Game Night for Guys & Party Night for girls Party: This is great if you have a big enough home! Do it on a day that there is a BIG sporting Event! All the guys in one room watching the game while the girls party in another room!

Seasonal Party Themes

KIDS Only! Secret Shopping Party! This is a great idea for EVERY holiday. Contact youth groups at church, schools, day cares etc. Stock up on current inventory! Invite the kids over to shop for a Gift for Mom & Dad for the holidays (Mother's Day, Father's Day, Christmas etc.) Add to the fun by getting cheap wrapping paper & some crafting supplies at the dollar store & have them make a greeting card too!

New Year, New You Party: This is a party that keeps the group together and coming back for regular meetings through the month. The new year everyone has resolutions they want to keep. Think how your company can help them meet their needs and start finding people interested in getting a group of their neighbors, co-workers and friends together to accomplish that goal. Start your own group if you can't find a hostess and everyone will meet new people and bond over their shared goal. For example a "biggest loser group that will all lose weight together. A "scrap or die group" to work on getting their scrapbooks caught up together, a "family night in sight group" to start making family meals more often, a "look good, feel good group" of women who want to start practicing relaxation measures to distress their lives. You will have a presentation at the first meeting and explain how your products can help meet their needs and be available for support and help through the coming months. For example if you are a scrapbooker trying to help people get caught up on scrapbooks you may offer a night out each month where craft tables are set up and the group meets to share ideas and work (with your products available each time to help!)

Sweet Treats for Lovers on Valentine's Day

Spring Cleaning & Home Organization Party

St Patrick's Day Party, Luck of the Irish

Beat The Winter Blues Party

Easter Party: Kids paint eggs or go on a back yard Easter egg hunt, while the adults enjoy a party focusing on Easter dinner meal planning

Beat the TAX Season Blues Party

Mothers Day Tea & Dessert Party

July 4th Summer Cookout Block Party

Red, White, and Blue Party: Have everyone come dressed in their favorite patriotic outfit. Serve Red, White and Blue dessert.

Christmas in the summer: When your Christmas products come out, offer a Christmas in the summer show to allow guest to start shopping early. That way you do not need to worry about a product being out of stock or on back order.

Back to School Party: If you sell items that back to school kids & moms can use this is a GREAT theme Party! Tupperware Has dripless tumblers, sports bottles, sandwhich keepers, snack cups, fruit lockers. lunch boxes etc. put them ALL ON SALE in August to attract back to school shoppers!

Halloween Costume Party

Halloween Sweet Treats Party

Planning a Healthy Full Course Holiday Meal 101

Beat the mall crowds and do your holiday shopping from the comforts of HOSTESSES home: Guests can do all their Christmas shopping without getting out in the crowds. Have them create a Christmas wish list also and tell them to drop hints to friends & family about it. When they call you, you'll know exactly what they wanted.

Holiday Baking with Children Party

Holiday Cookie Exchange Party

Secret Santa Party: Have guests make a list of 3 items below $25 each then have each guest draw a slip of paper and they have to BUY one of those items on that list for the Secret Santa pal without letting them know its her! Then you have a second half of the party in a few weeks when the orders come in and invite guests back to exchange their gifts & for them to try to guess who it was that was their secret Santa!

Trim-the-tree party: Have the hostess put up her Holiday Tree & dig out her decorations! You all have a tree trimming party & afterwards you can hold your REGULAR SALES party!

Secret Santa Office Gift Party: A lot of workplace offices these days do secret Santa parties & exchanges! I make up a list ahead of time of all items that we sell that are $12 and less and attach the list to the front of the catalog and ONLY demo those items! Guests are always looking for affordable gifts for their secret Santa office parties and you can help them find them!

Special Event Parties

You can incorporate those special events in your client's life into a fun party.

Baby Showers

Birthday Parties

Bridal Shower: Know someone getting ready to get married? Bridesmaids can throw a bridal shower that includes some of your party games & products. You may approach them ahead of time about each chipping in money for a joint gift for the bride. Or offer the bride a bridal registry!! Give the list to each guest, and the bride to be is bound to get the products she wants.

Batchelorette Party: Great for bath & body products and much more. Get some fun games and lavish the bride to be with attention.

Back to College or Off to College Party: Summer Cookout & Pool Party for College Girls!

House Warming Parties

Anniversary Parties

Family Reunion Summer Cook Out & Pool Party

Misc. Themes
The possibilities are endless!!!

Teeny Boppers Spend the Night Party & Facials: A great way to get young girls just starting to think about make-up and taking care of their skin. Have them make up a wish list complete with e-mail or contact info for her parents. You follow up with them after the show.

Patio Party: Have a party outside on the patio; serve nice tall glasses of iced tea.

Desert Party: Have each guest bring a desert and share their recipes.

Build your own Sundaes: Hostess provides the ice cream and the guests bring their favorite toppings.

Pizza Party: Host provides the basics & guests bring their favorite topping.

Wine & Cheese Party: Hostess serves wine and cheese. An all time favorite!

Italian Bistro Party: Hostess supplies the pasta and sauce (white & red). Guests bring their favorite ingredient.

Potluck Shows: Each guests brings a dish--chose the theme for the potluck-example each guest is given a country and she must make a dish from that country to bring.

Happy Hour Get Together: Hostess serves tasty adult beverages, and guests bring favorite appetizers.

Chocolate Lovers Party: Serve chocolate, chocolate, chocolate!

Pool Party: Hold show around pool, get a small plastic play pool and fill with ice and drinks. You might even have a swimsuit contest! (or encourage people to wear one and be cool) Great to combine with Pina Colada Party, Strawberry Daiquiri Party, Margarita Mania Party)

Saturday Brunches: while air is still cool, have a morning brunch or tea. exchange-bring favorite recipe and sample to share.

Summer sizzler: Have the guest bring their favorite way to cool down to the party and let them judge who is the coolest.

Creative Hat Contest: each guest creates their hat that they wear to the party, contest for the best hat.

Picnic in the Park or Candles in the Park: Hostess supplies picnic and we do the show out in the park.

Hawaiian Shirt Party: Each guest wears their favorite Hawaiian shirt, offer drink with little paper umbrellas; possibly get paper leis to put around each guest as they arrive.

Bring your own Nachos Party: Hostess provides the chips and each guest brings a topping.

Summer Salads: Ask each guest to bring their favorite summer salad recipe and exchange, maybe samples.

Sports: Decorate your table with your favorite sports teams themes and colors.

Garden Party: Have the show in some-ones garden have every guest wear their garden hat or big floppy hat.

June is Strawberry month: serve strawberry shortcake

Very Berry Party: Make berry desserts or berry topping for cheesecake or ice cream

Big Chicken Party: Great way to get know new neighbors who just moved in or if you just moved. Invite people you don't know or don't know very well.

BYOV Party: (Bring your own veggie: Make veggie pizza)

Treat your MOM Party: ONLY MOMS & Adult Children are invited! Enjoy a fantastic BRUNCH before the party!

Home Daycare Owners Party: Demo products that would appeal to daycare owners (toddler line.)

Cooking & Baking Basics Party: GREAT for older Teen girls!

The One-Hour Quick Cooking Party: Demo how they can make a QUICK, HEALTHY TASTY Meal in less than 60 minutes!

The Good Old Days Party: Have guests dress up in 1960s & 1970s party wear!

Italian Pizza Party

For Teachers Only Party

Sweet 16

Build Your Hope Chest Party Senior Girls Party: A lot of girls will be getting their own first apartment or going away for college so capitalize on all those NEW graduates!

Entertaining with Style Party

Food On the Go Party: Works well with Tupperware & Pampered Chef. Adults are always looking for ways to transport their food to work & back as well as packing lunch for the kids for school!

Shop for your Second Home Party: These days a lot of people have vacation homes, condos, cabins etc. and they need to stock that home too with housewares & goodies!

Beat the Refrigerator mess rat race Beat the Clock Party: (These are fun to do on the days that we have time changes here in the USA) but you can do them any time! You can set it up that if guests order within 30 minutes of the party starting they get a 15% discount, at 45 minutes it drops down to 10% and so forth!

Auction Party with your Cash & Carry Products or your Discontinued Stock!

A cut above the Rest Party: Great if you sell cutlery, food choppers, scissors or if you just sell stylish products!

Hip, Trendy & Chic Party: Great for those who sell clothing, accessories & cosmetics!

Whets New with <COMPANY NAME> Party: (Every time your company changes its main line catalog, have a What's NEW with xxxxxx Party!)

Ice Cream Social Party

Kitchen Cooking & Household Solutions Party

Book Club: If you love to Read why not form a Book Club in your neighborhood? This works well if you are with a Book Home Party Company such as Usborne.

5 Ingredients or Less party: Again, this is appropriate for Kitchen Types of companies

Multi-Consultant neighborhood party: Find other consultants who represent NON-Competing Types of products in your community. Get together and you all HOLD ONE BIG party! Really great idea to hold a few months before Christmas to offer guests chance to get their holiday shopping done early.

Party Swap: Team up with another Consultant & Swap Parties with her!

The "more" you bring, the "more" you get: The more guests or outside orders they bring, the more freebie gifts they get! This encourages HIGH party sales!

Delicious Deli Party!

Healthy Lunch on the Go

Mans Best Friend Party If you sell PET Foods & Supplies this is a GREAT theme party for you!

So there you have it, a huge selection of party suggestions that will get you thinking of many more. Create a list of the parties you offer and their descriptions and perhaps create several sample invites for the different parties. Put them all together in a "Benefits of Hosting Notebook" that showcases invites and descriptions of your shows. Display the hostess rewards on the front or back cover. You can pass this around for guests to look at while you are closing your shows out and meeting with each customer one-on-one to see all the different types of shows that you offer. Of course, the ideas may get them thinking too and they will probably think of one custom made just for them and their friends.

6

Party Games

Recruiting Games

Here are some great recruiting games to include in the show

Hold That Pose: Ask everyone to respond to these questions by following directions, precisely.

> If you have a car and know how to drive hold up your right hand.
> If you enjoy being around people, wiggle your fingers.
> If you have a phone and love to talk, hold up your left hand.
> If you have lot of_____ products, raise your left leg.
> If you like money, and want more, raiser your right leg.

Now pick one of the most enthusiastic people from those who have two hands and legs in the air. Have everyone else hold their position until guest comes up front. Then have the guest introduce themselves to the group and select a product you offer he or she wants to buy or has at home and have them demonstrate it. Tell them you have something special to talk to them about later. This is a great recruiting game. Give everyone a gift for being such a good sport.

Draw the Trip Game: My company is giving us a **Cruise** so I am playing a game to give me the chance to talk about the **Trip.** Give everyone a piece of paper...tell your guests to close their eyes and imagine that they are in your company and they have won the cruise. Keep your eyes closed and we are going to draw some things: First draw an island in the middle of the paper. To the left of the island, draw a ship. You are surrounded by water, so put some fish in the sea. This is St. Thomas, so put a palm tree on the island. It is a nice day, so put some birds in the air. That ship didn't get there by itself so put a sailor on the ship (can be stick people). He might get hungry so draw some coconuts on the palm tree. Sailors like to see where they are going, so put portholes in the ship.

Sailors like entertainment, so draw me on the island shouting and waving. It's a sunny day so put a sun in the sky. Now open your eyes...How does it look? If ... Your Island is in the middle-10 points Your ship is to the left of the island and not touching-10 points You have more than 2 fish- 15 points The base of the palm tree is on the island-20 points. More than 2 birds in the air-20 points. The sailor is on the ship and not swimming- 20 points Any coconut is on the tree- 15 points. Any porthole is on the ship-20 points. I am on the island-20 points. Now if the sun is to the left - 20 points To the right-15 points In the middle-10 points. Add the points... perfect score is 165
Modify this game to your destination place!

Ask Me About My Job: This game is a great way to get your guests thinking about joining your company. Get or make up some tickets. Tell your guests that for the next 3 minutes you are going to play "Ask Me About My Job". The first person to come up with a question will get 3 tickets, the second person will get 2 and every question after that earns one ticket. You will hear questions like "How long have you been doing this?" and "How many hours a week do you work?" Answer them as positively as possible. Good answers to the questions above would be "I've been doing this for 12 months and I've never had so much fun" and "I only work evenings and weekends because I want to be home with my kids". After the three minutes are up, tell you guests to hang on to their tickets. You will have another short Q&A session towards the end of the party (your guests will have thought of some additional questions by then). After that have a drawing for a small prize. This game is a great opportunity for you to teach your guests about your business and they may see how could benefit them.

The Recruiting Game: Have guests add their points as you read this story. If any selling you have done before, put down 10 as the start of your score! If you have a car and are able to drive, the thing you must do is just add 5! A little spare time will add to your score, for this you may add 15 more! If you like people and think they are grand, add 6 more to see where you stand. Add 10 points if you think parties are fun, and when you add this you are almost done. If you score the highest, it is plain to see, a **<insert your company here>** Consultant/Demonstrator is what you should be!

How Green Are You: Answer truthfully. The player with the most points wins.

1. Do you have a green house?

2. Do you have green paint?

3. Do you have green eyes?

4. Do you have on a green ring?

5. Do you have on green shoes?

6. Do you own a green car?

7. Do you have green on?

8. Do you have a green rug?

9. Do you have a green chair?

10. How much money so you have in your wallet? (money)

11. Do you own anything green from this company?

12. Are you green with envy, and would like my job?

How Green Are You? Answers

1. 10 points

2. 5 points

3. 20 points

4. 10 points

5. 5 points

6. 5 points per pair

7. 5 points

8. 15 points

9. 5 points

10. 10 points

11. 5 points

12. 15 points

13. 50 points

TV Game: Tell the guests you are playing a game, and give each a piece of paper and a pen. Tell them all to listen very well! **After you are done reading**, have them write down all of the TV shows that were in the story. The one with the most wins! I was THIRTYSOMETHING, living through THE WONDER YEARS with my FAMILY and my husband taking ONE DAY AT A TIME. We were doing okay, but THE FACTS OF LIFE were that we were not born with SILVER SPOONS in our mouths. Our savings were in JEOPARDY and we didn't want to be in debt for the rest of THE DAYS OF OUR LIVES. I finally told my husband, it's time to get out of THIS OLD HOUSE or at least make some HOME IMPROVEMENTS. I don't want to start a FAMILY FEUD but I'm YOUNG AND RESTLESS and I want to contribute to the family finances. It's time for me to GET SMART. Don't be THE CRITIC, I'm in search of AMERICA'S MOST WANTED job. FAMILY MATTERS to me and I don't want to miss out on the PRIME TIME with the kids by hiring THE NANNY. Your Company offers a great opportunity. THE PRICE IS RIGHT, with little investment! Part-time work with full-time pay! And WHO'S THE BOSS? I am! But could I get up in front of a FULL HOUSE of PERFECT STRANGERS for 60 MINUTES and tell people how to take home their BOLD AND BEAUTIFUL with Your Company's merchandise and become DESIGNING WOMEN?

Of course, I have experienced some GROWING PAINS, but soon I was able to spread my WINGS and watch my business BLOSSOM. Your Company has made me feel like I'm part of A-TEAM. I have GOOD TIMES at home with ALL MY CHILDREN. My family CHEERS when my weekly profit-check arrives!

Soon I'll FLY AWAY TO PARADISE...a dream vacation for which Your Company will pay. My husband and I will be like HONEYMOONERS again, sharing HAPPY DAYS in ANOTHER WORLD. Your Company may not be for everyone, as they say, DIFFERENT STROKES for different folks. But, if your are MARRIED WITH CHILDREN and have strong FAMILY TIES, I highly recommend Your Company to you.

How Well Do You Know Your Hostess? Give a piece of paper to each of your guests and have them number it from 1 to 10. Then ask them to answer the following questions. 1) What is your hostess's favorite color? 2) If she could have any vehicle, what would it be? 3) How many kids does she have? 4) What is her favorite hobby? 5) Who is her favorite actor? 6) What is her favorite animal? 7) What is her favorite TV show? 8) What is her favorite food? 9) What is her favorite scent or smell? 10) If you were in need of something, would your hostess give it to you if she can? After everyone writes down their answers (including the hostess), read the questions again and have the hostess tell everyone her answers. The other guests mark on their papers if they got it right or wrong. The person with the most right answers wins a small prize or discount on their purchase. You can change and rearrange any of the questions, but leave the last one in place. It provides a nice lead- in to mention that the hostess will get free product if they purchase a certain amount, and/or book their own parties.

Games to Introduce Your Products & Special Incentives

Left Right Game: This game is a great way to start a party, right before you go into your presentation. Pass out one or two small gifts. Tell your guests that you will read them a story and that they should pass the gift to the person to the right when they hear the word "right" and to the left when you mention "left. The person holding the gift at the end of the story gets to keep it. Here is the story: I left my house and was on my way to (insert hostess's name) house. But I soon discovered that I had left my directions at home, right by the phone! Well, I knew right away that I needed to have the right directions to (insert hostess's name) house, so I turned left and I turned left and I turned right and made my way back to my house for the right directions. Sure enough, there they were, right where I had left them, right next to the phone. Finally, I was on the right track. I arrived right on time and set up my (insert your company name) presentation right over here. You all arrived and sat down. I'm going to get right down to work and tell you about (name of company). I hope nothing will be left out. In a moment I'll show you our new line of (insert your type of products) products. If you left home with the intention of shopping for gifts tonight, you'll find we have the right gift for everyone. Think about upcoming birthdays and holidays, we don't want anyone left out. I'd be happy to help you find the right gift for that special someone. (Insert name of company) has a (insert number of days) – day return policy. When your merchandise comes in please check it right away. If something is not right please call me right away and you can be sure I will take care of it right away. You don't want to be left with something you are not 100% satisfied with, right? If you'd like to be a hostess and earn free and discounted merchandise, this is the right time for you to explore hosting a party. I'm enjoying being here with all of you tonight and I hope you are having fun, too. I know you can't wait to see if we have that special item you have been looking for, so without further delay I will get right to the point of this party, which is showing you our great products! So, there is really nothing left for me to do except congratulate the winner, right?

Wishing Well Game: Have each guest make out their wish list. Then ask them to create a tally as follows:

ADD 1 point for every item on your list

SUBTRACT 2 points if your list doesn't include a SL subscription (or pick your favorite company product)

MULTIPLY your total by 2 if I brought 1 or more of your wish list items in my kit tonight

ADD 5 points if you put the (hostess's favorite item) on your list (ask hostess prior to party)

ADD 5 points for the (product name) because it is featured on the cover of our catalog

ADD 10 points for the (product name) because it is the most expensive item in the catalog

SUBTRACT 5 points if your list doesn't include any of the (special collection name or product)

ADD 3 points for the (product name) because it is this month's
Hostess Special

ADD 2 points for the (product name) because it is this month's
Customer Special

ADD 5 points if your list includes a book or food item

ADD 5 points if your birthday is this month.

1. Bonus 15 Points…if you book a party today!!!

My guests love filling out the wish list and then I have it for reference for their birthday, anniversaries and other holidays. The husbands love the easy shopping and I get extra orders!! The winner gets a prize of my choosing or sometimes, depending on the season or holiday, I'll have a variety of prizes. For example, I'll have the winner choose from 4 Easter eggs. Each egg has a prize in it on a piece of paper such as 10% off any item they purchase or a gift I've pre-purchased at the $ store

Dirty Dishtowel: Call the hostess about 3 days before her party to see how many guests are coming. Of course she doesn't know yet…. Tell her you forgot to have her ask all her guests to bring their oldest, most worn out & worst dishtowel. The hostess then has an excuse to call everyone she invited to see if they are coming and if so, to bring their oldest dishtowel. The night of the party each guest shows their towel, introduces themselves, and tells how long they had the towel. The one with the towel that looks the worst wins the prize -- "a new dish towel". No real game to mess with paper, etc., and the dish towels are inexpensive to give!

Purse Game: Give everyone a piece of paper and pen. Let them know that you will be asking them to pull things out of their purse. When you say the item to pull out give them 100 auction dollars for that item. 1. A pen, Say, "Now you can fill out your order." 2. MasterCard, Visa or Discover credit cards "You can use one of these credit cards when you place your order tonight. I take cash and checks too." 3. Address Book "You can use your address book to make a guest list for your own show" 4. House Keys "You can use your house keys to open your home to friends and family so that they can have fun like we are tonight." 5. Car Keys "You can use your car keys to drive to the friend's home who books tonight." 6. Checkbook "If your checkbook contains checks, but not as much money as you would like, you can talk to me at the end of the party and I can help you put more money in there." 7. Calculator "You can use this to total your free merchandise that you would like my company to give you when you have your own party." 8. Pen "You will need this to write a letter to tell your current boss goodbye when you start your new career with my company." 9. Chap stick "You will need this to freshen your lips after you talk to everyone you know about your home party, so that you can receive $15 Free for every one you refer that does a party or turns in a brochure order. 10. Cell Phone "You need to call everyone you know to come to your show." 11. Having a purse. You deserve that just for packing all those things around.

The Banana Game: Have your guest bring a dressed banana - you might want to make it a build your sundae party, have the hostess provide ice cream and have everyone bring a topping for points as well. If you brought your own banana - $100 in auction money. If its dressed up- $100 If its dressed like a man-$500 If its dressed like a women-$100 If it looks like a animal-$300 If it has eyes-$100 If it has a mouth- $100 If it has hair- $100 If it has glasses- $200 If it is wearing a hat- $200 If its wearing jewelry- $300 If its speckled - $500 If its green-$200.

Book To Look: Give everyone an envelope that says book to look on the outside and tell everyone that they can open it at the end of the demonstration if they plan on booking a party. Inside I put either coupons or gift certificates for them to use at their show. Everyone is usually dying to see what they receive so they book a show just to see what they get.

50/50 Chart: Any person that places a $50 order has their name placed on a 50-50 Chart. (There are 50 squares on the chart.) A $100 order would get two squares. When the board is full, draw a number for the winner who gets $50 in free merchandise. That is $2,500 sales in increments of $50. You are only spending $50 minus the 40% commission. Call it a promotion to reward your loyal customers. Note: this reward is ongoing not just for one show so the customer may get called back a month or more later with the news that they won!

Ice Breaker Games

The Candy Quiz
Have each guest number their paper 1 - 18. Tell the guests that you are going to tell them something, and that they need to write the answer in terms of candy, a candy bar, or other candy.
Questions and Answers:
1) A famous trio? (3 Musketeers) 2) A Galaxy? (Milky Way) 3) Can't hold on to anything? (Butterfinger) 4) Twin letters? (M&M's) 5) To chuckle to oneself? (Snickers) 6) Before 1? (Zero) 7) A famous baseball player? (Babe Ruth) 8) A workers favorite day of the week? (Payday) 9) An Indian burial ground? (Mounds) 10) A joy to be around? (Almond Joy) 11) A rainbow of color? (Skittles) 12) They can save your life? (Lifesavers) 13) A planet (Mars) 14) What do you call this? (Whatchamacallit) 15) Superman's human name? (Clark) 16) A famous New York street? (5th Ave)
17)These Tamalies are great? (Lemon Head)
18) Don't be a sourhead? (Lemon Head)

Find Things By Letter Game: Have everyone get out her purse. Tell them that you will call out a letter. They will need to find something in their purse that begins with that letter, and hold it up. Give auction bucks to the first person that holds the item up. You can make your letters you ask for coordinate with something great about your company!

Double Dice: You will need some floor space for this one. Get everyone in a circle and place some wrapped gifts in the center, usually a number less then the number of guests. (Choose inexpensive gifts, small picture frames, votive candle, cute memo pad, etc. $ Stores have some great items for this game.) When wrapping, make the gifts attractive. Wrap in different size boxes, add color, bow, or unique wrapping to make them look pretty. Set a timer for as long as you feel you want the game to continue, this also would depend on the # of guests at the show. Give dice to hostess and have her roll, if she rolls doubles she gets a gift from the floor, guests continue to pass the dice onto the next person. Once the gifts are gone from the floor anyone that rolls doubles can take whatever gift they want from someone holding a gift. End game when you feel all have had adequate time to pass the dice. This has been one of the most requested games when I host a show that someone has either been a hostess or has attended one of my shows that have played Double Dice

Family Feud: It's the old favorite family game! Chose the answer that most fits and the person with the most correct answers wins!
1. Name a food that makes a lot of noise
2. Name a cartoon character
3. Name something a clown wears
4. Name something that you use to clean your teeth
5. Name a magazine with one title
6. Name a football player
7. Name something a kid wears in the winter
8. Name a popular month for a vacation
9. Name a type of cookie
10. Name something people do on a plane
11. Name a type of pizza
12. Name an actor whose first name is Tom
13. Name a woman comedian
14. Name an expensive car
15. Name an animal in the zoo

Family Feud Answers

1. Carrot
2. Mickey Mouse
3. Red Nose
4. Toothpaste
5. People
6. Joe Montana

7. Mittens

8. July
9. Chocolate Chip
10. Eat
11. Pepperoni
12. Cruise
13. Roseann Barr
14. Corvette
15. Lion

The Balloon Pop: Let each guest pick out a balloon from a bowl. Then explain, the first person to blow up their balloon, tie it, sit on it & pop it will win a free gift. This is a great ice breaker for any group; it gets everyone up and laughing.

Crazy Quiz
1. What 2 words have more than 100 letters in them? (Post Office)
2. What has 4 legs and 1 foot? (BED)
3. Where does Thursday come before Wendesday? (DICTIONARY)
4. What is the best invention for looking through walls (WINDOWS)
5. What has its heart in its head? (CABBAGE)
6. What berry is red when it's green? (BLACKBERRY)
7. What is the first thing a man sets in his garden? (HIS FOOT)
8. What is put on the table, cut & passed, but never eaten? (DECK OF CARDS)
9. Which of the presidents wore the biggest shoes? (THE ONE WITH THE BIGGEST FEET)
10. What is a good thing to part with? (A COMB)
11. What is the best way to keep a fish from smelling? (CUT OFF IT'S NOSE)
12. What never asks questions, but requires many answers? (DOORBELL)

Get To Know Each Other Game: This game makes for a nice icebreaker, especially if most of the guests don't know each other. It can also provide you some clues about who may be a potential prospect. Pass around a bag of M&Ms. Tell everyone to take as many as they would like. Quickly ask them to count the number of candies in their hand. Each person then takes a turn standing up and telling as many things about themselves and their family as they have M&M's. Of course no one is allowed to eat their M&Ms until they have had their turn.

Replace It Game / Appliance Game: Give each guest an index card. Ask each guest to write down an appliance, piece of furniture or other thing in their home that they would like to replace. Ask them to list 5 or 6 reasons why they would like to get rid of it. When they have all finished their lists, have them cross out the item to replace and put in the name of their husband (or their significant other). Now have each of them read their cards one person at a time. They have to say, "I want to get rid of _____ (Ron, Tim, Bill), because he is, and then list the five reasons. Example: Couch. 1. Old. 2. Ugly. 3. Too Small. 4. Wrong Color. 5. Stinks. Now have them change couch to their husband's name and when they read it, it goes like this: I want to get rid of Ron because he is Old, Ugly he's too Small, he's the Wrong Color and he Stinks. One lady listed a hot plate that she wanted to get rid of and one of her reasons was, when he got heated up you couldn't cool him down. (The ladies had a lot of fun with this.) One guest that used her cat as the problem thing said "Her husband coughed up fur balls and went potty on her bed." Have fun with this one.

Purse Scavenger Hunt or Let's Make a Deal: Remember that old game show, Let's Make a Deal? At the end of every show, Monty Hall would give audience members money for a specific unusual item. This is the same idea. Divide guests into teams of two or three, giving them a list of slightly unusual items, including a few "why in the world would you carry that in a purse?" items. Assign points to each item based on the likelihood that someone will have it. (a lipstick carries 10 points, a can opener 90 points). The team with the most points is the winner

Have You Ever...?: Have you ever done something from this list of silly things? If so, you score a point. How many points will you score? Read this list to all players. Score one point for each one you have done. The player with the most points wins. THE LIST: 1. Locked yourself out of the house? 2. Lost a member of the family while out shopping? 3. Put something unusual in the refrigerator? 4. Turned white colors pink (or another color) in the wash? 5. Gone away from your home and left the iron on? 6. Put your heel through the hem of a dress? 7. Had your zipper break in public? 8. Gone somewhere with two different shoes or socks on? 9. Remembered an appointment after it was too late? 10. Called a member of the family by another name? 11. Been ready to bathe and found no hot water? 12. Fallen up the stairs? 13. Gone shopping for groceries and discovered you did not bring any money with you? 14. Driven away from somewhere while a member of your party was still out of the car? 15. Dialed a phone number and forgot who you called? 16. Locked the keys in your car? 17. Got into the car to go somewhere and forgot where you were going? 18. Put something in the oven to bake and forgot about it?

Brainless Test: Score one point for each question answered correctly. 1. Do they have a 4th of July in England? (yes, they have 4th of July everywhere) 2. Some months have 30 days, some have 31. How many have 28? (they all have 28 days) 3.Why can't a man living in Montreal be buried west of Calgary? (Because he isn't dead yet) 4. Why should a pedestrian crossing the street always take vitamins? (To keep from getting run down) 5. How do you get down from an elephant? (You don't – you can only get "down", as in feathers from a duck) 6. How many of each kind of animal did Moses take into the Ark? (none... Moses didn't have an Ark.... It was Noah) 7. If you take 2 apples from 3 apples, what do you have? (You have the two apples you took, of course)

Buff Lifeguard Game: The fun is in drawing a lifeguard without looking at what you are doing. Draw a circle for his head. Draw a body (remember he is buff not a stick). Put a face on him. Give him arms. Draw seagulls. Give him legs. Oh we can't forget the muscles. Put some swimming trunks on him. How about sunglasses on his eyes? Draw a whistle around his neck. Draw his life guard chair beside him. Award points for face on head, arms and legs touching body, birds in air, etc. Whoever has the most point wins.

Name The Slogan Game: Have each guest number their paper 1 - 24 and then have them write their answers to the slogans when you read them. They will receive 1 point for every correct answer.
1) Just do it...Nike
2) Eat Fresh...Subway
3) When it rains it pours...Mortin Salt
4) It's everywhere you want to be...Visa
5) Finger Lickin Good...KFC
6) Good to the last Drop...Maxwell Coffee
7) Because you're worth it...L'oreal Hair Color
8) Built Tough...Ford
9) Squeezably Soft...Charmin
10) Let the sun shine through...Windex
11) Melts in your mouth not in your hands...m&m's
12) You've come a long way baby...Virginia slims
13) Strong enough for a man but made for a women...Secret Deodorant
14) For the times of your life...Kodak
15) Have it your way...Burger King
16) Run for the Border...Taco Bell
17) Fly the friendly Skies...United Airlines
18) Zoom...Zoom...Mazada
19) It does the body good...milk
20) We'll leave the light on....Motel 6
21) Plop,Plop...Fizz,Fizz...Alka Seltzer
22) Have you had a Break today...McDonald's
23) When you care enough to send the very best...Hallmark
24) MmmmGood!!...Campbell Soup

Thread Introductions: This is a great way for your guests to introduce themselves to the others. Once you have begun your party, tell everybody that you are going to pass around a spool of thread and that they are to take a piece "as long as they think they will need". They will begin asking ... "need for what etc." You smile and say, oh it could be for anything, just take a piece as long as you think you will need, and pass the spool. Of course they might think well whoever comes closest to going around their waist etc. Or if they see their closest neighbor sitting to them takes a real short piece, they will take a real long piece. After everybody has taken their thread, you tear off a piece and wrap it once around your finger and hold telling them they have to do the same and they have to talk about themselves for as long as it takes to wind the rest of the thread around their finger. Start by telling them about yourself and your business (so take a longer piece) It can get wild if somebody has taken yards of thread

The Vacation Game: Ask each guest to bring a picture from her favorite vacation. Then ask them the following questions about their pictures. 1. Is the picture in color? (If yes, 5 points.) 2. Was the picture taken in the last 6 months? (If yes, 15 points.) 3. Are there mountains in the picture? (If yes, 10 points.) 4. Is there a lake in the picture? (If yes, 10 points.) 5. Is there an ocean in the picture? (If yes, 10 points.) 6. Was the picture taken on an island? (If yes, 15 points.) 7. How did you get there? Airplane 15 points Train/Bus 10 points Car 5 points 8. Is there a landmark in the picture? (If yes, 20 points.) 9. Are there any people in the picture? You 10 points Family/Friends 5 points each 10. Is someone waving "hi" in the picture? (If yes, 30 points.) 11. Is someone in the picture riding a horse, camel, or elephant? (If yes, 100 points.) 12. Did someone accidentally appear in the picture? (If yes, 50 points.) 13. Did you have a stranger take the picture for you? (If yes, 25 points.) 14. Is anyone kissing or hugging in the picture? (If yes, 75 points.) 15. Was the picture taken on your honeymoon (1st, 2nd, 3rd, or whichever)? (If yes, 50 points.) 16. Did the person taking the picture accidentally get their finger(s) in front of the lens? (If yes, deduct 10 points.) After reading the 16 questions, go back and give points that correspond to their respective answers. Total the points to determine the winner.

Jingles: You read the following quotes and have the guest try and figure out where the saying came from. The one that guesses the most wins.
1) "Because I am worth it" ------L'Oreal
2) "Nothing says Lovin like fresh from the Oven"-----Pillsbury
3) "A little Dab'll do ya"------Brylcream (from the 50's)
4) "Get your Kicks on "-----Route 66 (from the 50-60's)
5) "You got the right one, baby"----diet Pepsi
6) "The Real Thing", or "I'd like to teach the world to sing"---Coca Cola
7)"Good to the Last Drop"---Maxwell House
8) "Mountain Grown"---Folgers
9)"_____ tastes good, like a cigarette should"---Winston, approx 60's-70's
10)" Taste the Rainbow"---Skittles
11) "Like sands in the hourglass, so are the _____"-----Days of our Lives
12)"Just Do It"---Nike
13) "Melts in your mouth, not in your hands"....M&Ms
14)" Mikey will eat anything"-----Life cereal
15)"_____ does a body good"-----Milk

Simple Attention Getter Game: Just read the following story and the ladies add or subtract for their answers. Provide small pieces of paper and pens to help them keep track during the story. Give a prize to the one with the highest score. "This is a rather peculiar game. It really does not have a name. It's simple to play as a game should be. You just do as you're told, you see So now if you'll please give me your attention. We'll put an end to this suspension In the end, whoever scores the most will receive a prize of which to boast Now since you're all fashionable girls, give yourself 5 if you have any pearls You may add 3 if your toes peek out, And earrings will give you 2 more to shout. Score yourself 5 if you show any red. Add 6 more for a curl on your head. Now before you think you are going to win take away 2 for each safety pin. Give yourself 6 if your pants are tight. Add 1 for a scarf which is just about right. Add 5 more if your shoes are black, and take away 3 for a zipper in back. Now count all your buttons, for each you get 2, and take away 1 for each button that's blue. Give yourself 5 if your heels are high, and why not take 10 for the green in your eye. 10 more points for a rose on your clothes. Take away 5 if you forgot to wear hose. if your husband you kissed today - add 9. If he didn't, subtract 12 - you're subject to a fine. This is the end for there isn't anymore. Let's see who is the lucky lady with the highest score."

The Lipstick Personality Test: The shape of your lipstick can tell you a lot about yourself. Take the test and see what your lipstick has to tell you!

SLANT (keeps close to the original shape) ... This sincere individual is somewhat reserved and a rule-follower. She dislikes attention, adores family and friends and likes a scheduled lifestyle. **SHARP-ANGLED TIP** ... This mover and shaker loves romance, glamour and attention. She's a high-spirited, outgoing gal who enjoys meeting people but is selective of friends. She knows how to make the most of opportunity when it passes her way. **POINT** (sharp angles both sides) ... Attracting admirers is no problem for this attention-seeker. This shape is a sign of elegance and good taste and this woman loves all the finer things in life. Count on her being faithful and spiritual. **CONCAVE** ... This inquisitive, restless and adventurous type makes a great detective and attracts friends easily -- probably due to her sincerity and generosity. She's torn between tranquility and adventure, and although exciting, she can also be complex and serious. **FLAT** ... The shape reflects a straight shooter who is determined, ambitious and reliable. She dislikes superficiality, has high morals but she does tend to be a bit impatient. **DULL POINT** ... This lovable, family-oriented woman has a mind of her own and is a doer working best under pressure. She loves having people around, but tends to have a bit of a stubborn streak and exaggerate sometimes. **CURVED** ... Money is the name of the game and this woman manages her finances well. Add to that loving, affectionate, energetic and talkative, plus this creative type tends to be a people-pleaser. **ROUND** ... This methodical, hard worker knows exactly what she wants out of life. She's even-tempered and makes a good friend because she's considerate, steady and generous. Count on her to be an animal lover, as well as a peace-maker

Alphabet Letters Game: Have guests list 1 – 15 and give them the following clues. The answers should be a letter of the alphabet. The one with the most correct will get a prize!
1. A girls name..... K(kay)
2. An insect....... B (Bee)
3. Body part...... I (Eye)
4. What Fonzie says... A (AAAA)
5. Body of Water...... C (Sea)
6. (Fill in the blank) Wiz G (Gee)
7. Vegetable..... P (Pea)
8. A refreshing beverage..... T (Tea)
9. Opposite of me..... U (You)
10. Marks the spot..... X
11. A boy's name..... J (Jay)
12. A real bad grade.... F
13. An Expression...... O (Oh)
14. A question....... Y (Why)
15. What would happen if you cloned yourself ...... W (double you)

Games to get them Listening to your Presentation

Interactive Presentation Game: As with any activity, you have to determine if this would suit the group you are working with. This activity does not use equipment, so it is easy to do on the spur of the moment.

I introduce the activity by telling the guests that I need their help. I teach them actions or sounds to make when I say key words in my presentation. These are rather silly, of course, but this encourages guests to listen for key words. Choose only about five actions or sounds so it does not get too complicated or long.

For example:

"14kt gold", they say "oouu"

"jeweler" - they say "bing bong" (the sound of the door bell when the jeweler arrives)

"hostess" - they applaud or say "thank you!" when they recognize a hosting benefit, they say "aahhhh"

"Swarovski crystal" - they are to shade their eyes (from the brilliance of the stones!)

"Moose Jaw" (the home of Fifth Avenue Collection), they put their fingers on top of their heads to represent moose horns.

"bonus gift" - "whoopee"

"book a show" - touch the side of their head and say "hmmm"

This can be easily adapted for your presentation.

Customer Demo/Recruiting Game: Type up descriptions of whatever merchandise you have out on your display. You can also use the descriptions right out of the catalog and 'doctor them up' a bit.
Cut the descriptions into strips so you have one per strip. Also do the Customer monthly sales bonus, Hostess monthly bonus and some recruiting information. Have each guest pick one as they enter the party. (You may want to coach each person a bit if you like, i.e., show them the item and talk about it a bit). After the introductions, have each guest "demo" their item. This is a great way to see which of the guests would be a good consultant! You could also try for spring parties, using plastic Easter Eggs in an "Easter Basket". Halloween parties using the small plastic pumpkins; and Christmas you could use the small stockings….etc…

Blue Light Special: This is fun for everyone. Set timer and demonstrate your product. What ever item your holding when the timer goes off is on sale for the duration of the party.

Bingo: This is an easy all-time favorite and an easy way to introduce a wide variety of products to the group. Create some bingo cards by drawing a 4 by 4 box grid on a piece of paper. Write "Free" on the center box. Then write the names of your products on the remaining boxes in random order on each of the bingo cards and make yourself a set of cards with just one of the products on each card. You will use this set of cards to draw the bingo "numbers". You may want to have a sample of each of the products with you and show it and talk about it when the product is drawn during the bingo game. As in ordinary bingo, the first person who has a row of items checked off wins a prize.

The Price Is Right Game: This game offers an alternative and fun way to describe some of your products.

First, choose products you want to highlight. You'll need 1 for the first "item up for bid;" 3 for the first "pricing game;" 1 for the 2nd item up for bid; 1 for the 2nd pricing game; 1 for the 3rd item up for bid; and one for the 3rd game.

In between games 1 and 2 will be a "Commercial Break" and in between games 2 and 3 will be a "commercial break."

Ask for 3 volunteers to bid on the first item. Give each a ticket (I use tickets and draw one winner at the end of the show; others use auction dollars) for volunteering. Describe your first item. Ask each to guess the actual price without going over. The closest wins. Award one ticket for winning; 2 tickets for exact price guess. The winner plays the first pricing game. This game is "Which two?" or "Same Price." Describe 3 items—two of which have the exact same price—and ask the player to guess which two are priced exactly the same. Award one ticket for an incorrect guess and two tickets for a correct guess.

1st commercial break—guests ask you questions about your hostess program. Award a ticket for each question.

2nd item up for bid—if enough guests, ask for 3 new volunteers. If not enough guests, replace the winner from game 1 with a new contestant. Describe your next item. Winner plays the 2nd pricing game—"More than or Less than." Describe one of your items and state an incorrect price for that item. Ask the player if the actual price is "more than or less than" the amount you stated. Award one ticket for incorrect answer and two tickets for correct answer.

2nd commercial break—guests ask you questions about your business opportunity. Award a ticket for each question.

3rd item up for bid—repeat #2 process. 3rd pricing game—"higher or lower." Describe an item and have the player guess the price. You then tell her if the actual price is higher or lower than her guess. Keep doing this until she gets it right (it's the "clock game" on the TV show). Award two tickets for getting right price.

I don't do a 3rd commercial, but you could with a general question session or whatever you want to cover.

Seasonal Games

Valentine Puzzle: Buy children's Valentines and cut them into about 5 or 6 pieces, making sure all of them are in an envelope. Pass an envelope to each guest. With the starting signal each empties out her puzzle and puts it together. The first one finished gets the prize!! Variation of above...Cut large red cardboard hearts in 5 of 6 pieces jigsaw style. The group of 5 or 6 who first completes a heart wins.

Pat-In-It Game: All of the answers contain the word "Pat." 1. Boy's name Patrick 2. Girl's name Patricia 3. Highway Policeman Patrolman 4. Something an Inventor needs Patent 5. You need this to make a dress Pattern 6. You sew this over a hole Patch 7. Another word for pitiful Pathetic 8. A person who loves their country Patriot 9. Where you have a barbecue Patio 10. One who discovers a new way Pathfinder 11. A baby's game Pat-A-Cake 12. Type of quilt Patchwork 13. Rapid talking or rain on the roof Patter 14. Small road, lane or way through the woods Path 15. Shiny shoes Patent Leather 16. Ruler or head of a family Patriarch 17. Hamburgers Patties 18. Self-control or endurance Patience 19. Person who frequents a place of business Patron 20. Fatherhood Paternity 21. World War II General Patton 22. Delicacy made from goose liver Pâté 23. Pat that mends Patch 24. Loves his country Patriot 25. Does sentry duty Patrol 26. That the doctor welcomes Patients 27. That is a kind of quilt Patchwork

Easter Egg Game: Here is a game to play with all of those left over plastic eggs you will have after Easter :) Take six plastic eggs and fill each one with a little gift (use your imagination) In 3 of the eggs write "Congratulations! You have won a **Insert your company here** show!!!" Seal the eggs with tape and put them in a basket in full view of everyone. Before you award your door prize and give your Hostess credits that evening ask if anyone likes to gamble. If so, maybe she would like to take a chance on winning something. Tempt your guests by telling them that their chances of winning are 100%! Tip: Make sure your guests understand that if they choose an egg they must be willing to book a show with you.

Right/Left Bunny Game: Wrap a present in a box and as you read the following story, the guests will pass the present according to the directions, either LEFT or RIGHT! The winner is the person holding the present at the end of the story! "Once again Easter is RIGHT around the corner. Peter Cottontail is working himself RIGHT up to losing his

LEFT whiskers, not wanting a repeat of last year. On the night RIGHT before Easter, RIGHT before everyone LEFT the chocolate shop, Peter stopped RIGHT in front of the LEFT-hand door. He wiggled his LEFT ear, then his RIGHT, twitched his RIGHT whiskers, then the ones on the LEFT. Something was not RIGHT. The basket of Easter eggs was missing! You had all stolen them! Everyone panicked and went to look for it RIGHT away! They looked LEFT, RIGHT, LEFT, then RIGHT again. It was nowhere to be seen. Peter was not going to give up RIGHT yet. It should have been RIGHT where he LEFT it! Those eggs needed to go to all the boys and girls on Easter morning. Suddenly Peter's RIGHT-hand bunny remembered RIGHT where he had LEFT it. RIGHT to the LEFT of the beginning of the bunny trail. So, on Easter morning Peter Cottontail hopped LEFT, LEFT, RIGHT, LEFT, RIGHT, RIGHT, RIGHT down the bunny trail to deliver baskets full of Easter joy."

Jelly Bean Game: This one is for Easter but you have to be careful when you have children at the party, because they scream and cry for jellybeans. Have each guest choose 5 of their favorite jellybeans and then award points for each color they choose. Pink-4 points. The hostess keeps the pink copy of the order so she knows what you get when the order comes. Blue-5 point. You will not feel blue when you book a party today. White-8 points. Your Designer enters you order from this copy, directly into the company computer. Yellow-6 points. Keep the yellow copy of the order as your receipt. Black-10 points. You will be in the black when you earn as a **Insert your company here** Consultant Green-12 points. The color of the money you can earn when you become a **Insert your company here** Consultant. Red -subtract 8. Work your way out of the red, become a **Insert your company here** Consultant. Orange-7 points. Orange you glad you came tonight? Most points wins prize.

Here Comes Peter Cottontail: Give each guest a paper plate and a pencil! Have them place the paper plate on top of their head and give them the following instructions:
A circle for their bunny's head
Another circle for his body
The bunny's right leg
Oops, give your bunny a left arm
Gee ... we only drew one leg ... now draw the left one
And while you're at it, give him his right arm too!
Now, Peter needs a face ... give him one please
Don't forget his whiskers and ears

How about putting an Easter basket on the ground next to him
Just in case he gets hungry, put a carrot in his left hand
Now, put some eggs in his basket
OH NO … we forgot his fluffy cottontail, please draw one!
And last but not least, write Happy Easter at the top of your page!
Score as follows:
5 points if his face is in the circle for his head
5 points if his head and body touch
10 points if the tail touches bunny at all
25 points if they decorated the eggs
20 points if at least 2 eggs are in the basket
50 points if the carrot is in his hand
5 points if the carrot touches Peter at all
5 points if the basket is near his feet, and not in the air
5 points if you can read Happy Easter
Highest score wins a prize!

Mother's Game: Name the famous mother who: 1. Was the first "First Lady"-----------------Martha Washington 2. Made the first flag--------------------------Betsy Ross 3. Her cupboard was bare---------------------Old Mother Hubbard 4. Joined the Peace Corps at age 70-------Lillian Carter 5. Her husband was a civil rights leader----Coretta Scott king 6. Her husband was shot at Ford's Theater-Mary Todd Lincoln 7.Became an artist at age 70-------------------Grandma Moses 8. Mom to J.F.K-------------------------------Rose Kennedy 9.Princess Diane's Mother-In-Law--------------Queen Elizabeth 10.Mommie Dearest----------------------------Joan Crawford 11. You don't mess with her------------------------Mother Nature

Red, White & Blue Trivia: Have the guests guess correct answer "red, white or blue" 1.. Stop Signal ... Red Light 2.. President's Home ... White House 3.. Fib ... White Lie 4.. Nursery Rhyme ... Little Boy Blue 5.. Porter At A Train Station ... Red Cap 6.. Robin ... Red Breast 7.. Moby Dick ... White Whale 8.. Architect's Plan ... Blueprint 9.. Famous Song by Irving Berlin ... White Christmas 10.. Luncheon Special ... Blue Plate 11.. K-Mart Special ... Blue Light 12.. Famous Brothers ... Blues Brothers 13.. Large Waves ... White Caps 14.. Toronto Baseball Team ... Toronto Blue Jays 15.. Valentine Symbol ... Red Heart Let the games begin!

Getting In The Holiday Spirit
1. Name a holiday carol with 4 words in the title.
2. How many types of Christmas cookies can you remember?
3. Name one of Santa's Reindeer?

4. How many days are left until Christmas?
5. Write a small holiday tip that always helps you through the busy season.
6. In "Twas the Night Before Christmas" who was not stirring?
7. Name a Christmas Flower and Christmas Green.
8. Name a Holiday Greenery with human anatomy in the word.
9. Name 6 common items you would see on a Christmas card (like sleigh, Santa Claus, etc)
10. Name your favorite Holiday Tradition or custom.

Answers:

1. Joy to the World, Away in a Manger or any others with 4 words only. Have guest give one point if answered correctly.
2. The guest with the most varieties of cookies gets the point here. Any type of cookie made at Christmas counts.
3. Dasher, Dancer, Prancer, Vixen, Comet, Cupid, Donner, Blitzen, Rudolph (any one of these; guest gets one point)
4. 14 (only one answer here...and one point)
5. Any answer here gets a point.
6. Not even a mouse (one point for correct answer)
7. Poinsettia, Christmas Cactus, Boxwood, Holly, Mistletoe, etc. (one point for correct answer, but you must have both)
8. Mistletoe (only one correct answer here...one point for correct answer)
9. Christmas tree, holly, snowflake, snowman, ornament, gingerbread cookie, candy cane, star, angel, Nativity set, toy sack, gift, etc, etc. (must have 6 to get a point.)
10. Any answer here gets a point.

Have guests add up points and give prizes for: MOST POINTS, MOST INTERESTING HOLIDAY TRADITION, MOST HELPFUL HOLIDAY TIP, MOST VARIETIES OF COOKIES, LEAST AMOUNT OF POINTS

Christmas Trivia Game: 1. Finish singing: You better not shout, you better not cry.....Answer you better not pout I'm telling you why, Santa Claus is coming to town. 2. Who first sang "White Christmas"? Answer Bing Crosby. 3. In Holland, they don't have stockings to fill, what do they fill instead? Answer: Wooden shoes. 4. On what weekend does Santa arrive at most malls? Answer Thanksgiving. 5. In Mexico, what do they say for the greeting "Merry Christmas?" Answer Feliz Naiad. 6. Finish singing: On the first day of Christmas my true love gave to me: answer A partridge in a pear tree. 7. If you've been bad, what will Santa leave in your stocking? Answer Coal. 8. Finish singing:" All I want for Christmas is".... answer, "My two front teeth. 9. The U.S. Post office suggests you mail all packages and cards for US delivery by Dec 25th on what date? Answer Dec. 10th. 10. Recite my favorite." twas the night before Christmas and....answer all through the house not a creature was stirring not even a mouse. 11. Continue...."I in my kerchief and ma in her cap had just settled down for a long winters nap. 12. I'm red and white and taste good as can be, you can find me hanging on the Christmas tree, I look awful pretty, I'm so tall and thin, a peppermint is my next of kin! What am I? Answer Candy Cane. 13. Who is the most famous reindeer of all? Ans. Rudolph. 14. What is the name of the little girl who wondered "is there a Santa Claus?" answer Virginia. 15. In the Miracle on 34th street, what did the little girl wish for the most? Answer a house. 16. There are 365 days in the year, what day is Christmas day on? 359. 17. How much does it cost to mail a Christmas card? answer 39 cents. 18 In 2000 what day of the week does Christmas day fall on? Answer, Monday. 19. How many days apart are Christmas and new years? Answer, 7. 20. Who "stole" Christmas??? Answer The Grinch

7

Treat Your Business Like A Business

This is YOUR business! You have to treat it like a business to be successful. The problem for most people is that although the initial cash investments are low, the time investment is much more than they expect. The majority of the people who start a home party sales business are women seeking part time income. Many are mothers of small children who have chosen to stay home with their children. They want an outlet all of their own. They are attracted by low start up costs and the opportunity to "get away from it" for at least a few hours a week. But if they are not careful to use that small amount of time they have set aside for their business to the best advantage, they are setting themselves up for failure.

So many consultants spend time trying to reinvent the wheel. That few hours a week that they envisioned working on the business can quickly turn into a full time job without full time pay. They become overwhelmed by trying to get everything rolling at once and despite the time they invest, they end up getting nowhere. This leads to the new consultant feeling disgruntled and disillusioned by the company and consultant that signed her up. Without a doubt this is the quickest path to failure, so start off on the right foot by focusing all your energy on the very most important key to your new businesses success: establishing relationships with clients. Faithful clients will not only lead to reorders and possible repeat hostesses, but your most loyal client is often your best recruit

Schedule a time each week when you will work on your business without interruptions. Spend that time establishing relationships and following leads. Give extra service and time to good customers---they will be repeat hostesses and potential customers.

Keep an address book of past customers and hostesses to help keep in touch. Use post cards, newsletters, or e-mails to inform clients of monthly specials, new products & catalogs. Don't forget to mention new hostess specials, incentives, and challenges. If there aren't any, make one up!

Make sure to keep good notes about your clients to help with follow up. Remember their favorite product line or special requests they may have made and jot a personal note on your monthly newsletter telling them if their product is on sale that month. Remember their birthdays by offering a special month long discount.

Encourage frequent customers to regularly plan shows. At the show, encourage the hostess to rebook a show in 6-9 months. She'll be the first to see and try new products. Don't forget to follow up with anyone who has said maybe, sometime, or seemed interested at the show but did not book. They may decide later to have a show. Either call or send them a card saying something like….

Dear Susan,

Thanks for attending Elaine's home party. I know you were interested in hosting a show and thought of a theme that I thought would work great for you. You may also be interested in a "Pass the Catalog party. I want you to earn free merchandise like Elaine who earned $125 in free products!! Please keep me in mind for this or for reorders.

Hope to hear from you soon!

Keep Good Record for Big Savings Come Tax Time

Keeping track of your business expenses lets you know how you are doing in your business. Plus it can add up to big deductions from personal income come tax time. Your business income less business expenses gives you your taxable net income. The more expenses you track, the less your taxable profit. So maximizing your expenses could lead to big deductions on personal taxes.

Most of the costs of doing business can be deducted. You can deduct for mileage while delivering products, donations given as prizes in contests, and proceeds from charity parties given to charity. Some examples of less obvious deductions that are allowed include: cost of samples, advertisements, bad debt, printing, postage, internet connection, office supplies, web page hosting, hostess gifts, entertaining costs for open house, and traveling expenses (including amounts expended for meals and lodging other than amounts which are lavish or extravagant under the circumstances) while away from home in the pursuit of a trade or business.

Remember the "laugh test." Can you put down the expense for business without laughing at putting one over on the IRS? For example, some direct sellers erroneously think they can decorate their home with products and deduct the cost as a business expense. To be deductible under IRC Section 162, the expense must be an ordinary and necessary expense paid or incurred in carrying on a trade or business. As soon as you start using a product for personal reasons, it is not deductible. Even if the product will occasionally be used as a sample or to demonstrate to potential clients.

At the end of the year you will need to fill out a Schedule C. A professional tax accountant or CPA is an expert at all of the confusing tax codes and usually pay for themselves with the loopholes they find. Also, their services are a write-off. You will still need to keep good records during the year to bring to the accountant in order to claim greater deductions. You will need to bring them the following information to help maximize those deductions: Gross Sales for the year, Inventory purchased over the year, ending inventory value, all expenses including mileage which will be calculated as a dollar amount on a separate worksheet and added to schedule C.

Leave a paper trail. The IRS wants you to keep business records separate from personal. Make sure your business doesn't look like a hobby—get business cards, advertising materials and print & keep monthly & annual cash flow reports. In addition to the info needed to fill out schedule C, you should keep receipts & track business expenses. Keeping all of these important records doesn't have to become a full time job! You need to spend time where it counts---establishing relationships with your clients. Home Business Makeover has developed a low cost software program called "MY HOME BUSINESS" that is customized to home party sale consultants. They have several versions that come with pre-filled information for your company. This one of a kind program **tracks clients, leads, hostess lists, upcoming shows & events, inventory, cash flow, profits & losses, and tracks tax related expenses** so you'll have everything in one place come tax time! All your business information is stored and tracked in one convenient easy to use program. You can even try it before you buy it at homebusinessmakeover.com. I highly recommend this business tool--- I use it myself every day!

Establishing good relationships with your clients is your number one goal. They are the road to all of your other business goals. From them you will get lifetime clients, hostesses, and hopefully future consultants. Good luck with your new business. The sky truly is the limit, so go reach for the stars!

Made in the USA
Lexington, KY
30 May 2014